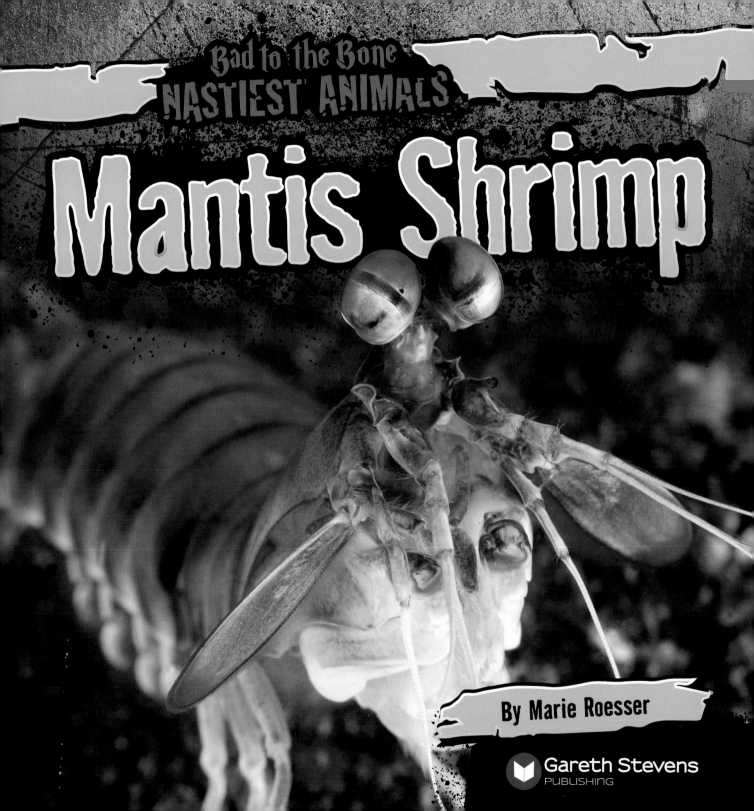

Bad to the Bone
NASTIEST ANIMALS

Mantis Shrimp

By Marie Roesser

Gareth Stevens
PUBLISHING

Please visit our website, www.garethstevens.com. For a free color catalog of all our high-quality books, call toll free 1-800-542-2595 or fax 1-877-542-2596.

Library of Congress Cataloging-in-Publication Data

Roesser, Marie, author.
 Mantis shrimp / Marie Roesser.
     pages cm. — (Bad to the bone. Nastiest animals)
 Includes bibliographical references and index.
 ISBN 978-1-4824-1958-0 (pbk.)
 ISBN 978-1-4824-1957-3 (6 pack)
 ISBN 978-1-4824-1959-7 (library binding)
 1. Stomatopoda—Juvenile literature. 2. Crustacea—Juvenile literature. [1. Crustaceans.] I. Title.
 QL444.M375R64 2015
 595.3'796—dc23
                         2014024261

First Edition

Published in 2015 by
Gareth Stevens Publishing
111 East 14th Street, Suite 349
New York, NY 10003

Copyright © 2015 Gareth Stevens Publishing

Designer: Michael Flynn
Editor: Therese Shea

Photo credits: Cover, p. 1 Stubblefield Photography/Shutterstock.com; cover, pp. 1–24 (series art) foxie/Shutterstock.com; cover, pp. 1–24 (series art) Larysa Ray/Shutterstock.com; cover, pp. 1–24 (series art) LeksusTuss/Shutterstock.com; p. 5 Ethan Daniels/Shutterstock.com; p. 7 Adrian Kaye/Shutterstock.com; p. 8 Eric Isselee/Shutterstock.com; p. 9 (inset) Dorling Kindersley/Getty Images; p. 9 (main) nitrogenic.com/Shutterstock.com; p. 11 Daniela Dirscherl/WaterFrame/Getty Images; p. 13 Reinhard Dirscherl/Visuals Unlimited/Getty Images; p. 15 worldswildlifewonders/Shutterstock.com; p. 17 Andrea Izzotti/Shutterstock.com; p. 19 Dai Mar Tamarack/Shutterstock.com; p. 21 John A. Anderson/Shutterstock.com.

Printed in the United States of America

CPSIA compliance information: Batch #CW15GS: For further information contact Gareth Stevens, New York, New York at 1-800-542-2595.

Contents

Words in the glossary appear in **bold** type the first time they are used in the text.

Beware the Mantis Shrimp!

What's the most dangerous animal in the ocean? Could it be a shark, killer whale, or octopus? For a number of sea animals, it's the mantis shrimp! That's because this little creature is lightning-quick with its **weapons**—two large claws.

There are more than 350 kinds, or species, of mantis shrimp. They're usually small, so people don't have to fear mantis shrimp. However, they were given the nickname "thumb splitters" by people who've experienced the power of their claws!

That's Nasty!

A mantis shrimp's claws are so strong that they've been known to break aquarium glass!

Mantis shrimp can be beautiful colors. Some are less than 1 inch (2.5 cm) long, and others are longer than 1 foot (30.5 cm)!

Crusty Crustacean

Mantis shrimp are crustaceans (kruhs-TAY-shunz). Lobsters, crabs, and crayfish are all crustaceans, too. Like other crustaceans, mantis shrimp have several pairs of legs, two antennae, and eyes at the end of **stalks**.

Mantis shrimp aren't actually shrimp, though they look similar. Mantis shrimp are a kind of crustacean called a stomatopod (stoh-MAH-tuh-pahd), which means they have gills on their **abdomen**. Gills are a body part that fish, crustaceans, and other sea animals use to breathe underwater.

Mantis shrimp usually live near coasts, but are also found in deep waters.

Shrimp Smash!

Mantis shrimp got their name from the bug called the praying mantis. That's because one pair of the mantis shrimp's legs are much larger than the others. They look like the front legs of the praying mantis.

These large legs have claws, an **adaptation** that gives the mantis shrimp its deadly skills. When the claws aren't in use, they're folded under the shrimp's head. However, when the claws are **extended**, things get dangerous for the mantis shrimp's prey!

praying mantis

That's Nasty!

The praying mantis is known for being nasty. Females sometimes eat their **mates**!

Besides their large claws, mantis shrimp have three pairs of walking legs.

Smashers and Spearers

Mantis shrimp are placed into two groups, depending on how they use their deadly claws to hunt prey. One group, the smashers, uses their claws to smash through the hard shells of **mollusks**, such as clams and snails.

The other group, the spearers, use sharp claws to stab fish and other tasty sea animals with soft bodies, like worms.

Both groups can attack their prey about 50 times faster than you can blink your eye! That doesn't give prey much time to run away.

This mantis shrimp has captured a tasty meal—a clam!
It'll use its claws to smash through the shell.

Fast Moves

Mantis shrimp are incredibly fast. Some say they're the fastest predators on the planet! A mantis shrimp can move its club-like legs at about 75 feet (23 m) per second! Scientists think they can strike so quickly because their claws are wound like a spring.

Moves this fast make hot gas bubbles in the water. When the bubbles hit the mantis shrimp's prey, they can be shocked or even knocked **unconscious**. That's like getting hit twice with one punch!

That's Nasty!

One thousand milliseconds make up 1 second. Mantis shrimp can stab their prey in 20 milliseconds!

Mantis shrimp can smash their prey even faster than they can stab.

Swimmers and Burrowers

Some mantis shrimp wander the ocean floor looking for food, while others hide in **burrows** and don't come out often. Smashers use burrows under rocks. Spearers burrow into sand. Mantis shrimp are excellent swimmers and swim up to grab their prey.

Divers can sometimes hear groans coming from burrows. This may be male mantis shrimp calling for a female mate. The sounds may also be a warning for others not to come into their territory. The shrimp "hear" with tiny hairs on their body.

That's Nasty!

A mantis shrimp may seal the opening of its burrow with **mucus**!

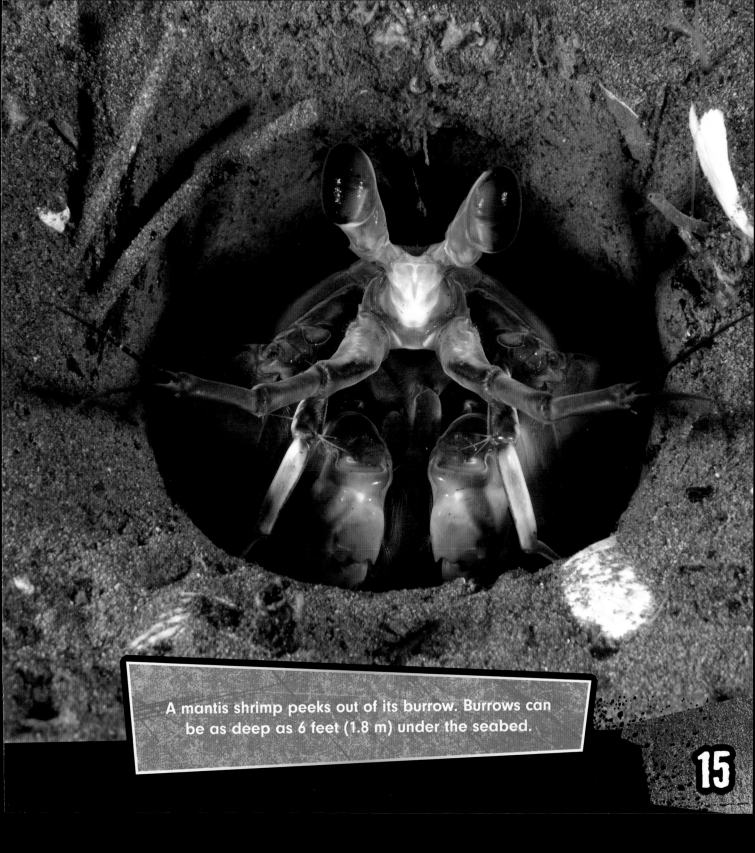

A mantis shrimp peeks out of its burrow. Burrows can be as deep as 6 feet (1.8 m) under the seabed.

15

A Mantis Shrimp Family

Most species of mantis shrimp live alone. However, some stay with their mate for their whole life, which can be more than 30 years, and the two may share a burrow. The male sometimes hunts prey for the female and brings food back to her.

Females lay many eggs at one time. The group of eggs is called a clutch. The female keeps them in the burrow. She may lay another clutch that the male takes care of.

That's Nasty!

Even young mantis shrimp **plankton** have claws to hunt!

When mantis shrimp eggs hatch, they may spend about 3 months as plankton and float around until they're fully grown.

Incredible Eyes

Scientists have been very interested in studying mantis shrimp eyes. They can see many more colors and kinds of light than we—or any other animal—can.

Their eyes might help with their lightning-fast hunting. When humans see something, a message goes to our brain to tell us what it is. Our brain may then send a message to our body to move. A mantis shrimp's eyes tell its body if what it's seeing is something to hunt or to fear. Then the shrimp can make its move.

A mantis shrimp's eye is larger than its brain!

Aiding the Ocean

You can eat different kinds of mantis shrimp, but people are trying not to catch too many. That's because mantis shrimp play an important role in the ocean. They keep the numbers of some sea creatures in check by attacking and eating them. They also stir up the ocean floor, which keeps the water healthy.

Mantis shrimp are also a good way to tell if there's too much pollution in the water. When mantis shrimp are healthy and fighting, the ocean is a healthier place!

excellent eyesight

lightning-quick movements

great swimmers

Mantis Shrimp: So Nasty!

tough claws for smashing

sharp claws for stabbing

Mantis shrimp may be an ocean nightmare for prey, but they're truly amazing animals!

Glossary

abdomen: the part of an animal's body that contains the stomach

adaptation: a change in a type of animal that makes it better able to live in its surroundings

burrow: a hole made by an animal in which it lives or hides. Also, the action of making such a hole.

extended: stretched out

mate: one of two animals that come together to produce babies

mollusk: an animal that lacks a backbone and has a soft body, such as a snail, clam, or octopus

mucus: a thick slime produced by the bodies of many animals

plankton: a tiny plant or animal that floats in the ocean

stalk: a slim support for a body part

unconscious: unable to see, hear, or sense what is happening because of accident or injury

weapon: something used to cause someone or something injury or death

For More Information

Books

Brynie, Faith Hickman. *Which Animals Are the Best Athletes?* Berkeley Heights, NJ: Enslow Publishers, 2010.

Kenah, Katharine. *Tiny Terrors.* Columbus, OH: McGraw-Hill Children's Publishing, 2004.

Websites

Mantis Shrimp
australianmuseum.net.au/Mantis-Shrimp
Discover some other names for this crustacean.

Mantis Shrimp
www.chesapeakebay.net/fieldguide/critter/mantis_shrimp
Check out some fun facts about the mantis shrimp.

Peacock Mantis Shrimp
www.aqua.org/explore/animals/mantis-shrimp
Read about this species of mantis shrimp.

Index